Would You Like a Poem?

By Maria Dios

Copyright © 2014 Maria Dios
All rights reserved.
ISBN: 061587598X
ISBN 13: 9780615875989

Table of Contents

1 - Writing

3 - Polishing Shoes

9 - Stroll

11 - Tracks

15 - Water

21 - View of the Harbor

23 - Ghost

27 - Dance

29 - Catch Me

33 - Linoleum

39 - Wolf

45 - Bridge on the Turnpike

51 - Cape Cod Memory

59 - The Charles in Winter

61 - Winter

65 - The Shower

69 - Houses

73 - Orbs of Light

79 - Relativity and Paradox

83 - Venezia

89 - The Emerald Sea

93 - Medicine for the Millennium

Would You Like a Poem?

Writing

oh how we scheme and design

with those uncanny patterns we call words

not to create

but if we could only embrace

what was gleaming in fascination and exquisite delicacy,

sifted through experience and perception

from the very drollness of human life

and in spite of that

being hopelessly compelling

how does it do that?

and why is it always hidden

yet alluring and enticing the helpless

to exude it through the very blood

and life stream of consciousness

and when it's done,

to gloat in the infinitesimal victory

as though one were a god

Polishing Shoes

Tin jar with dark striped rows

round and dangerous to touch

I'll get it on my fingers and nose

the stuff smells strong and such

an oiling creamish substance spreads

across the leather

(not the sole).

I hold my shoe closely in my hand

and turn it angled slightly down

the rag I use was cast but now

how clothey feels it in my grasp

as I'm coloring in and feeding well

the little scars and cracks.

This shoe wore me a lot this year,

a good shoe and though it lacks some newness

well revives in poetry

since on me it's waited, walked and danced,

skipped, tripped and fallen

artfully

from the sole of my foot

has taken shape

my arched curve it knows intimately.

With even strokes and doting power

I lavish on the polish,

increasing tone, full-bodied and restructured,

resilient shine, (note the subtle design!)

how the leather grain is textured.

Jar of tin returns to shelf

and cloth behind the basement door

shoes well indulged valiant return

pressing coupled against my feet

to support the many small delicate bones

and the details I oversee.

Stroll

Misty summer evening stroll

where I am precious cargo

on a sidewalk cracked and rowed

each tree a large hand

guiding me on to the next

with generous and scented sweeps

sprinkling me with roses

or tricycles

or hoses

whatever the specialty of the yard

may be

Tracks

I get the Sunday paper

and park along the tracks

where the old wrought iron points

starkly, rusted

and the heavy track is dark

edged around by stones

in winter's bare plight

branches poke through the fence

the paper recounts other events.

Water

Water is blue green ocean vast and deep

Water is for scrubbing the bathtub with comet

Water is for baptism and devotions

Water is for drinking – 8 glasses a day

Water is for sinking the enemy

Water is for swimming, for surfing, for races

Water is for soaking feet in tired places

Water is for life – fish and fauna at sea

Water is for gazing at the shoreline

Water is for artists, waves rising majestically

Water is for fountains, for wishing, for glee

Water is for miracles, Bethesda and Lourdes

Water is for turning into wine by Jesus

Water is for recipes, pasta and rice
    boiling, sautéing, and making ice

Water is for cooling hot machinery

Water is for dissolving and making tea

Water is in clouds, in rainfall and floods

Water makes electricity

Water makes suds

Water is 90% of the human body

    and the principal part of fruit

Water is for children's amusement in the pool and down the chute

Water is in bottles, cans and plastic jugs

Water is in glasses, paper cups and mugs

Water washes out dirt in the clothes

Water goes out in the dryer

Water is one thing of which

    our need is dire

View of the Harbor

I see my white sneakers with toes up

as I relax on this old wooden bench

and lean back in the curve that's built in

and my posture is lost, that's the point

for I am no longer myself

when I gaze at the harbor beyond

the water looms large

its lapping takes over

the sounds of the world are estranged

the mist and the air and the water

concoct inarticulate symphony

I hear it in my nerves and my bones

like stings of violins powerfully

while their rhythms massage me

while they mercifully wash me clean

Ghost

My therapist is in complete denial

that I could ever have seen the eerie smile

of a strange tall woman, darkly clothed

who wandered in my childhood home

who circled the dining room table at meals

at dinner, mostly, round the din of five voices,

she floated, I remember no feet, nor the sound of heels

but she looked at me grimly, and my little sister squealed,

"Who is that woman? Why does she leer at you so?"

Though I was used to her questions,

the answer I did not know.

We let her pass 'round us, we hadn't any choice.

She never said anything, it seems she had no voice,

but some dark sullen anger, she vented toward me.

At least my sister believes me, the hell with therapy!

Dance

the beat's

surge comes up through my feet,

with the heat of an Indian chant

grasping with relief the words voice cannot reach

donning the body of ingenious mind

that is all mine for a time

hugging closely its rhythm

embraced in its strange jubilation

detaching me so expediently from the tedium of the mundane

and even the pain of old love

is loosed by its' passion

though again and again I find it there hiding

dissolves away in the essence

one day I will look and find you there scarcely

will I miss you my long beloved enemy?

Catch Me

I'm standing in a place

that has no name

where I balance

on air so delicate and

sweet

just me

do you see the silken movement

of my feet as I create this dance

far away

from pain

yet still close,

so close, like slipping

through the cracks

it's an art, I learned it somewhere

it's in the way I move and breathe

the way I set my mind at ease

and more that that

I hear

a musing note in breeze

spell binding lyre

enchantment like whipped cream on top of grief

it's an unknown art

in a glance I'll be there -

catch me!

Linoleum

when I got my first kitchen

it had a linoleum floor

and I'd wax it

that keen aroma sprinted through the house

the celebrated glassy gloss

someone would say in lilted voice

"you waxed the floor today!"

they have no-wax floors today

they shine all the time

polished

like women in suits and big earrings

with crimson manicured nails

well heeled and striding ahead

in business

but they are not light enough on their feet

to dance on the kitchen floor like me

and would never condescend to wax

or understand

my love affair

with linoleum

Wolf

O wolf

you have long been my magic

I saw you first as black wolf

even in the dark night in my room

near my bed you were by me

You were there in the blackness

when my lover turned against me

into his own darkened madness

you were dark and far more beautiful then

You bring to me to a rare silent place

enlightened with bright seductive magic

your glistening fur

the scintillating points of stars in a dark sky

each one

a dazzling moment of truth

coming close to me

charged with this sleek force

that I crave beyond my own species

your eyes focus distantly

yet directly into mine

deep and sweet

neat

and leap far beyond time

into the primal creative fires

landing four paws square

How can your blackened nose

and semi smiling lips

bewitch me so?

face of beast

so intelligent, so crafty, demure

puzzling, generous

appealing, enthralling, poised,

solid,

pure,

wolf

Bridge on the Turnpike

Lattice of green metal overhead

    lacey against blue sky

        delicate geometry hovering above

            tires below hitting hard pavement

                with sounds of metropolis

                    industry,

              crowds,

            a thousand vehicles passing below

        the spidery green fingers above

    hold steady,

touching,

    unknown or unheeded with

        its mathematical lore

            bridging city to city

                yesterday to tomorrow

            bridging daily commute to homeward trek

        or playtime to tragedy

    or loneliness to love's onset

bridging perhaps the bonding of men

    in a world moving onward fast

        to a place backward in time

            where every man stores one memory

              at least

                  of a moment of peace

                      in the midst of mankind's
                      continual battle struggle
                      and tug

        bridge looks like magic

    afloat on high

  look up and under

its fingers write against the sky

Cape Cod Memory

Alabaster sand dune with tufted green growth

wild and majestic against azure blue

embedded through time

I ignored you, buried you, denied your sublime

and vibrant voice, textured resonance,

healing current washing over mine -

now your sandy white fills me with space

like wind expanding huge tents,

unfolding creases, cleansing air blowing out corners

flapping relaxation and the mirth of nowhere,

your green tufts so simple, so rooted,

all my harried details are booted off

to refuge with the grace of this intoxicating clump

wildness

growing on the dune

not to leave soon

nor ever

its dense outline determinedly grows

on my mind

forsaking all other matters

unabolished in the azure

waving on the clearness

The Charles in Winter

the Charles winds moodily around the land mass

      wavering dark ribbons of glass

         a million odd stars on a moonlit planet

secret glowing crystals hidden in the water's depths

       a sub conscious mind terrain

    the black bass keys on a piano

      striking deep chords,

moving out of the past,

         close as an arm's length

Winter

Winter's coming on

with its canopy of shadows

pierced by glaring morning suns

and bright nightfall moons

mixed palettes in the sky

peaches, purples, blues and pinks

with clouds looming larger

so much time is darker

my bed is more important

books and pillows and tea cups

my couch is strewn with blankets

soup simmers in a pot

many hats and gloves and socks

I'll get through it, I'm able

I admit I like it a lot

hibernating and wearing pajamas

lighting candles and cold fresh air in a gust

the quiet outside, the privacy, the stillness

I like being expected not to do much

I forget how much I like winter

when the bare trees

in their naked exotic shapes

agree to stay with us

The Shower

My disappearance is complete

when finally I draw my feet

across a step of tile into

the sacrosanct flood of water.

Water beats upon my head

and I oblige as one half dead

in this my private interlude,

to be laid upon its altar.

A thousand hushing voices shout

my griefs and woes they all come out

the syncopation strong and bold

drives them to the drain.

dross sullen lifts away from me

and cleansed, I feel bright energy

exhilaration, tap on skin

my spirit poised to soar again.

Houses

houses sit in rows

houses sit on hills

houses get bigger

houses get old

houses are repainted,

redecorated and sold

houses can be vacant

houses can develop mold

you will remember

the house where you lived

the sun in the bedroom

the door in the wind

the squeak in the staircase

the wallpaper in the hall

the distinctive scent of the basement

the mirror with a flaw

houses hold love

houses hold sorrow

houses hold what enters our souls

and in our bones become marrow.

Orbs of Light

These great orbs of light

came out of nowhere

like beings from other worlds

undoubtedly they are about me

and with dignity move,

in bold declaration,

negating denial

why yes, they are beautiful

and why not declare love

whether I choose to or not

these orbs that sprung from my soul

and have a life of their own

a light of their own

too many to extinguish

I'll leave them alone

and enjoy their distinguished,

exclaimable,

redoubtable,

paroxysms

of

love,

brilliant and serene

beyond time, above hope, beyond anything I've ever known or seen.

Relativity and Paradox

Einstein was Jewish

but he went to Catholic school

He was German

but he disowned his country

He was a genius

but he didn't' speak well until the age of seven

and his first teachers said he'd never amount to anything

That's when his father gave him a compass and he said

the needle must be attracted to some invisible force in space

In his youth he was rebellious and flippant at authority

but he never became one

they say he had dark hair and blue eyes and had a way with women

but when he married it was to a peasant woman who was intelligent and open minded

He loved to talk with his friends but had little use for society

He was content to pursue his bliss

He worked in a patent office recording other's inventions

to keep the wolf from his door

and in the evenings solved the puzzles of the universe

in a small apartment in Bernes, Switzerland

Eventually he discovered relativity

He put up with jealousy among his peers

He made the bomb possible

but he didn't approve

He knew more than anyone

but he said we can hardly know anything

and that it was enough for him to wonder at the mystery

He said we all come into this world for a short time

and leave it without really knowing why

Venezia

The Venezia I visited

was so silent, an un-city

where I stayed in an old Duomo's home

with no elevators

its front door floated out

on a dock with lights strung

where you could sit at night

in the un-ruined darkness

sprinkled with dots of

old chandelier light

and soft melting reflections on water

accompanied by the melody of lapping

before finally climbing the stairs

slowly and higher to your room

all tile, Venetian glass and carved furniture

that had it's own say

with its shuttered windows looking out on a courtyard

all gated and potted with flowers

that even in the daytime

was content

with the only sound of steps

falling now and then on stone

The Emerald Sea

Would you go with me

to the Emerald Sea

and lie on a blanket

(absorbed in a book) where

sun dapples brightly

through leafy shade trees

that lend us their scent

and their magic?

Will you go with me, quietly

and stretch out your body

with blades of grass

tickling our feet

and be drenched in the moment

while the cosmic blue lake spreads above us?

Or nuzzling earth sideways

we'll visit with ants

who loyally ambulate harmlessly

we don't have to speak

just a glance, or a sigh

a sweetness descending between us

a dog barks somewhere

a child cries excitement

we are gifted a rapturous rest

the green ocean's humming

our heart strings are buzzing

afloat on the Emerald Sea.

Medicine for the Millennium

some kind of pieces

some translucent petals

are falling

      out of the cosmic heaven

through the stratosphere of earth

      through the cold air

falling alike on the many greedy

      and on the many needy

Their substance is unearthly

like the manna we've only imagined

shall we touch them, ingest them?

      shall we store them or crush them?

shall we boil them, inject them?

      dissect them, convert them?

perhaps to inhale them

with a deep breath and hold them

'til they burst into light in our consciousness

with knowing

nevertheless

they keep falling and snowing

we cannot ignore them any longer

they're glowing!

Illustrations:

1-Writing

2-Polishing Shoes – Sketch by Maria Dios – mdios333@live.com

3-Stroll

4-Tracks- photograph by Tom Conklin – taconklin@me.com

5-Water- painting by Laura Craciun – laurawhitewing@yahoo.com

6-View of the Harbor

7-Ghost- painting by Dolores Dios – doloresdios@gmail.com

8-Dance

9-Catch Me

10-Linoleum – photo by Maria Dios

11-Wolf

12-Bridge on the Turnpike – photography by purchased and permission of artist whose name was lost in a computer crash; will the author of this photo please write to me if you see this photo and I will add your name to this page.

13-Cape Cod Memory – painting by Laura Craciun

14-The Charles in Winter

15-Winter

16-The Shower – Sketch by Maria Dios

17-Houses

18-Orbs of Light

19-Relativity and Paradox

20-Venezia –painting of a painting (artist unknown) by Maria Dios

21-The Emerald Sea

22-Medicine for the Millennium – Colors by Maria Dios

www.ingramcontent.com/pod-product-compliance
Lightning Source LLC
Chambersburg PA
CBHW042337150426
43195CB00001B/19